Compositions of the Dead Playing Flutes

with much love,

love,
B

Compositions of the Dead Playing Flutes

POEMS BY
Barbara Ellen Sorensen

ABLE MUSE PRESS

Able Muse Press

www.ablemusepress.com

Printed in the United States of America

Library of Congress Control Number: 2013945189

ISBN 978-1-927409-23-7 (paperback)
ISBN 978-1-927409-24-4 (digital)

Cover image: "Flutist for Shape Dance" by Alexander Pepple

Cover & book design by Alexander Pepple

Able Muse Press is an imprint of *Able Muse:* A Review of Poetry, Prose & Art—at www.ablemuse.com

Able Muse Press
467 Saratoga Avenue #602
San Jose, CA 95129

For Bryon Michael Sorensen
(b. May 8, 1987 – d. October 29, 2011)

Acknowledgments

I am grateful to the editors of the following journals where many of these poems originally appeared, sometimes in earlier versions.

Barefoot Review: "Valley of Fire," "Sky Islands," "Water from Oar."

Copper Nickel: "Pictographs," "Weathered."

Cutthroat: "Song from the Deep Middle Brain."

Mangrove Review: "Descending Aria."

The Mountain Gazette: "Sweetgrass and the Art of Bicycle Maintenance."

The Pedestal Magazine: "Observing the Museum's Montage," "Story from an Iñupiaq Sewing Kit," "Desolate Beauty."

Wazee: "Some Small Thing I Have Held," "Twins," "Taking Pleasure."

Women Writers of Haitian Descent: "Dance of Manna."

Eight of the poems appeared in the chapbook *Song from the Deep Middle Brain* (Main Street Rag, 2010).

I would like to thank Alex Pepple and Able Muse Press, including all their fine readers, for turning this manuscript into a book.

Foreword

In her poem "Desolation Beauty," Barbara Ellen Sorensen writes, "Into this fragile landscape I place my story." The several fragile landscapes she explores include the natural world, the interwoven human fabric, and the body each of us inhabits. In this poetry, fragility is recognized, but with it an attendant persistence. Both qualities become radiant in the poet's regard and resonant in her mouth.

Poetry can record many things, one of them the journey of a soul abraded and burnished by life. This book—fierce, tender, accurate, and full of grace—is such a record. As it explores realms of loss and grief, relationship and solitude, and body and spirit ("the other close world"), it does so with restraint and fullness, in language both spare and rich. There is an earned fearlessness here that will catch in your throat, then carry you deeper into this work.

The travel sack of necessities for any life journey holds words. These words call the poet's world into being. *Compositions of the Dead Playing Flutes* is rooted in such words. The poet's lexicon includes the tactile world—ice, wind, sand, soil, water, desert, ocean, garnet, rose, and tundra—for the natural world is central here. It includes such words as struggle, dream, longing, lift, and torn—for the poet experiences the world deeply. Ancient voices speak here, from layered time and from within the poet. In these lines, one such voice speaks from within:

I'm filled with a disease that's moving me
to a center that may be as cold as snow,
and I will arrive there gratefully.

Flesh is essential: body, limbs, tremor. Birds enter: heron, sandhill crane, hawk. Emotions breed motions: climb, hold, fly, dance. Here is desire, and there, longing. Here is gratitude. Astonishment. Opening. Beauty. Dreams. Wounds. Medicine. Disappearance. And love.

These poems are attentive, scrupulous, and transforming, as they range from the sensuous to the spiritual. In "Sweetgrass and the Art of Bicycle Maintenance," the poet writes of a young man fixing her bicycle:

He was so beautiful, I was afraid
to speak. If I opened my mouth,
yew berries, little mariposa souls
would have rattled out instead of words.

In "Wing Medicine," she considers her illness: "When the body is beginning/ to weaken, it pays attention/ to the creature it hopes to become." Of the loss of a son, she writes, "Unbearable, unbearable your death." Yet she also knows this of the dead: "...we do not keep them, they keep us torn, in love, and again, in love."

The poem "The Lovely Feast" describes being opened—in what the poet names "the fierce baptism you had been waiting for." Opened in body and spirit, the poet embraces her worlds, and she offers back this poetry, which shimmers in its urgent, delicate balance.

—Veronica Patterson

Contents

I
WIND, WATER & MEDICINE

II
WINGS, CREATURES & OTHER TALES

III
BOUQUETS, FEASTS & FLUTES

Compositions of the Dead Playing Flutes

I

WIND, WATER & MEDICINE

In the high barrens
The light loved us.

–W.S. Merwin

Pictographs

My children first opened their eyes inside the ivory petals of the yucca.
I can touch the claretcup's flower and disarm its needles.

I found my sister's earring beneath a juniper tree.
A hurricane carries shells from the ocean floor to the desert.

Once when I was small, a hurricane carried away all my dolls.
It is warm at the top of a hurricane;

all of my dolls lived to tell me this.
My children too, were born with inner springs. Malleable.

My sister's children are ancient as pictographs.
They hold hands in rows across slickrock.

Some of these children were torn through suction.
A hurricane is an inverted suction.

The juniper tree and the yucca plant are related
and by their waterless roots,

you can watch river water turn to gold in the desert.
My children disappeared in the desert.

I found their footprints in the cryptogamic soil.
Where there is no water you think of hurricanes.

Deserts and children are fragile; they change shape as you breathe.
All the water in the world threatens to fill their lungs.

Endymion's Shadow

Windward on the river
we found Precambrian rocks:
layer upon layer of ash-black languor,
flecks of cricket wings
chirring around them.

From the raft, my sister and I
could see the quiet houses
of swallow nests,
thickened rock dove nests,
molded upside down
on the ridges above.

Moon stretched pale
in child's pose.
Fifty stars gave birth
to fifty daughters.

Plum trees lined shores
and herons turned
their diurnal circles.

We slept on sand
and the black rocks
pressed down over us
with their hushed,
timeworn shoulders.

We were carried
through dreams easily,
no one grown old or sick,
no one ever leaving.

Hitchhikers

For Sean

The boys who wander this highway
appear when rain stretches out tourmaline

black, a thin knife between
their mothers' hearts and the river,

their footprints trailing down
the canyon. Sometimes they hitchhike,

their silent shapes emerging for seconds,
dissolving quick as snowflakes,

their spirits resonating
through the chasm they have never left.

Everything they ever loved keeps changing.
The living forget how they looked and

what they would have been
and the arroyo takes pity and swells with a sound

some can hear if they wake at night and listen
for the footsteps of boys returning with roses

and ribbons on the birthday of their deaths.
Once when I was driving this stretch

of two-lane highway through mares' tails,
I saw the boys risen too soon. I called to them

as if their necks had never been broken, as if the only
membrane they ever fell through was not glass

or metal, but the soft, yielding tissue
of lovers who go on conceiving them

over and over until they spill forth,
once again flesh and bone.

And, called, they rushed
to the center of the road made white

from spring snow falling,
their lost wholeness close enough

that I could see them standing stark,
and sparkling.

Early Winter Field

Red sky dredges
up a weak moon.
I study midden, leaves,
and brittle yucca that rattles
when I touch its husks,
sound of soft-seeded cachos.

Rime-frosted and perishing,
leaves form asemic shapes,
lines of vascular tissue so delicate
and perfect I can no longer
bear to crush them
beneath my feet.

In a parched field,
I can always find what I love.
Near wetland grasses,
blue verglas veils a pond.

I run my hand across it
and a winter fantasia breaks
open, absorbing the song of sparrows
refusing to migrate.

Here, I have found
wind-scattered music,
the instruments of water,
a primeval chorus
preserved in ice.

How Snow Fell

When I was a girl,
there was a star magnolia
tree and its blossoms
covered the ground
with a pale pink opacity
outside my mother's
bedroom window.

Once, I found long blades
of timothy grass, and thought
I heard a *maat kheru,*
a voice calling
forth the lost. The thin reeds
of grass stood sharp,
defining the vibration of whirling
life within montane meadows.

By the sea, I watched foam flushing
out the two-hearted
soft ones, sometimes a whelk shell.
I wanted to place my hands over them.

In autumn, corpses
of leaves were hastily
herded, the great piles
of heady fragrance

sending seraphic bodies
of ash into the air.

I looked up
to watch the slow wave
of near-winter sun
move with resonance
across the yard.
Knowing snow
would come next, I learned
to make all things
diminishing, sacred.

Sky Islands

I dream my youngest son walks
with me to the edge
of a teal-colored alpine lake
sparking blue embers,
reflecting only that I may
have imagined his
entire existence.

I dream the epiphany of frost
hushed across cottonwood branches,
in early spring, the very day
he came to me.

I dream of bells, cornflowers,
and the effervescence
of bodies being born to dream;
of undulations, and how the Maya
blue sky remembers
my son's journey even when
I have forgotten.

I dream I am beside a tarn that holds
one boulder tumbled
down from fields of many,
and that the act of its falling
has clarity, as if in falling
it creates a line, a scar as blue

as the cord from which
my son floated, whole, perfect.

I dream my son dances
on some far land,
his young body moving
from space to space, valley to valley.
I see him beside
midnight blue lakes where
he beckons, radiant.

Valley of Fire

The day you died
I was photographing
red yucca, little-leaf sumac,
fire barrel, lace, and rainbow cacti.
Smoketrees backlit
with sunrise flared,
branches busy with the rising
inflection of snowgeese.
Asters pressed against New Mexico's
alabaster sand and sunset
swept over the bright yellow
amplitude of rabbit brush.

You were dying, though I did not hear
or feel you. The dissonance
of death was in everything;
everything could have been you:
abrupt shadows threading
between sun-bleached wooden crosses
in a graveyard resonating
with charms and votives.
The silence of the deaf
in the Valley of Fire,
ebony lava furrowing
furiously across the land.

Wings, wings,
your body must have pled,
as it struggled with its seizure.
Nothing heard you,
not even birds. There was no warning,
just restless scratching
through air. There were no birds
that could have carried
you that day, even with their
upward-arched formations
across invisible miles,
back into my womb,
giving you breath,
my heart's desert willow
beating full with air.

Dance of Manna

After ecstasy of rain-wash
on a red clay road in Petit-Trou-de-Nippes,
a woman weaving
through a crowd of *rara* dancers
knelt to rub a white cotton
cloth into the earth.

She wiped it across her face,
then rose to caress
my face with it as I swayed
in near-dusk light,
all the words of missionaries,
their warnings,
passing into the pale
emptiness from where they came.

She spoke lovingly
to the earth in Creole song.
Around her clanged the deep
sounds of steel pipes molded to trumpets
and elongated horns.

Startled from sleep
on lemon tree perches,
hundreds of egrets
lifted into the air.
As they flew, I danced
as though I was the *loa Ayizan*.

I danced as though my body
was pounding out
red bone-marrow sound,
yellow bone-marrow sound.

I danced as a goat tied
to a tree bleated,
then opened its throat
to a machete. Its blood
drained innumerable miracles
into a wooden bowl.

Sometime during that night,
a young Haitian man brought
coconuts, calabash, citrons
and laid them by the opening
of my tent.

In the morning, I was alone
on the land, a wilderness
of wind against me.
Where was the woman
who wiped my face
and blessed me?
I let the fruit go to waste,
to the black flies of morning,
denying the dance of manna, balm.

Near Huntington Beach

A pool is perfect architecture
6 a.m. in yellow light.
Under wave clouds and rain
I float on my back
and gaze at flowers,
birds of paradise,
their namesake treasured
hundreds of years ago
for brilliant skin,
their feet severed from their bodies.
In this southern California city,
they are transformed again
into nervous decorations
like everything else.
I am still floating
breathing in the sea
where the evening before
I bent and rose on a beach
collecting mussels, stones.
The pelicans had surprised me.
Here in the pool, I search
the sky knowing they
will never come into a city, but wishing
I could study once more how
their charred shapes
swam the air in tight geometric form.
Then suddenly, one

separated from the
others, folded
to a sharp point
and upside down plummeted,
pulling color with it,
all the sunset singing
as it drew down its wings and beak
to puncture slippery fish—one or two
lifted a tiny heart
close to the surface
as I am now, swimming backwards,
hearing a distant siren,
thinking how white
salt spray must be welcoming the day
in equal brilliance
flushing out everything to be consumed.

The Lost Trinket

From a far shore,
I watched a girl
enter the water,
watched as her charm
bracelet slipped
from her wrist
as she was pulled under.
Some women reached down
and wrested her
from the turbulent
currents of the sea and I thought,
she must feel as though
she is dead. The sun
was hard on her back.
The women were laughing
and smiling down at her;
they knew she hadn't gone far.
One of them squatted down
beside her, and her father
came rushing through hot sand.
Moments after
she had swallowed salt water,
I knew everything
would be different for her
now that her silver charm
bracelet had been pulled
far out into the ocean,

caught by tangled seaweed
to remain immutable
and tarnished.

Song from the Deep Middle Brain

When everything around me tremors,
why should I be still?

Emerging from my left
side came this palsy,

my arm transformed
into a frangible branch of cold leaves

wavering, made slow, heavy
by evanescent wind and ice.

I closed my eyes and it was still
there in morning's bracelet light

that slid down my arm,
down to my fingers,

as though many synapses
spoke gibberish to one another,

unaware they were
sinking fast as sound

slips from ocean shelf to slope,
to rise, then, irretrievably from the plain.

My father's hands shook, Anya said,
as she manipulated my body

through warm water.
She held me up and her fingers

caressed each vertebra,
and I bobbed as if atop a wave,

a pale, scarred fish.
When I was a little girl in Poland,

she began her story,
we had to cross a border

and there were men demanding our papers.
My father could not open them

because his hands shook,
and his papers fell like the pappi

of dandelions onto a frozen ground.
Why are you shaking they asked him,

searching his face for lines
that might transmogrify it.

I am a child of war, he told them.
At this, they laughed and laughed,

but let us pass.
Why did they laugh, I asked.

Anya shrugged and said:
You see, many things can cause a tremor.

I stretched under her
steady healing hands

as they coaxed my limbs
to release an invisible pain.

She knew of places in my heart
where I would eventually come to rest,

once I had learned
what children of war learn:

how the body submits
to absolution so it might again float.

Ghostflower & Wind

The hundred diseases develop from wind.
    –from the Huángdì Nèijīng

We spread our bodies
naked across sandstone
in late afternoon,
lie down to feel
the way the stone's curvature
lifts our fragile ribs,
the way the wind blooms
imperceptibly across our bones.

Later, wandering,
we find a cow's skull
disintegrating, the earthy salt
of its composition
becoming transparent,
wind by wind.

We bathe by our tent's bent spine.
Water overflows
from a small bottle
warm over our faces.
The desert's pumice
beneath our feet scrapes away
the hushed, age-old dust.

When we are clean,
the wind comes again,
discordant ringing
bell. Our shadows string
flat along iron-red walls,
our alabaster stomachs become
charcoal rubbings.

I trace hers with my eyes
as she lifts
her heavy black hair,
watch as her hips move
like a lily slide, a wedding of bones.
When I raise my arms
she says, startled: *Look,*
your left hand is shaking.
Does it hurt?

I serenade her with a vision:
we were searching
for a desert ghostflower.
We searched ravines until we found it.
Yellow stamens flaring
outward, visible
from slopes and washes.

When we found it,
she saw how sturdy it was,
realizing, then, how it bargained
with the wind every day
for its harsh existence.

Debutante

The hair stylist helps
me pick a cut that will cradle
my scalp,
a lace veil. I watch
as thick layers
of hair fall
in tufts. She stops
cutting periodically
to sweep around her feet. I am sitting
up straight, thinking: *drill bits,*
screws, saws. All
of these instruments
will be used in the operating theater,
where I will be
a profound and sleepless act.
Finished with cutting,
the stylist hands me
a mirror. Under midday heat,
with my lightened head
exposed to sun,
I decide my toenails
need polishing, my feet
massaging, and wonder
how I will manage
to remove this nose piercing,
not allowed
in the operating theater.

Words drift
down like ashtree pollen:
frontotemporal, parietal,
temporal, suboccipital.
I touch my head,
feeling the tight,
smooth haircut
I have just been given,
and picture vulnerable
organisms clinging
to tundra surface
with all the strength
they can conjure:
moss campion, chiming
bells, snow
lovers, orange lichen. The wind
dwarfs them without mercy,
its applause deafening
as it builds
in momentum to swoop
down, like a scalpel intent
on making the perfect incision.

Resident Gryphon

The Simorgh is inherently benevolent and unambiguously female. Being part mammal, she suckles her young.

–Shahnameh (Book of Kings)

What if, during deep brain
stimulation surgery,
I looked up at the neurosurgeon
who had drilled one perfect hole
in my head, and awakened me
from sedated sleep so I could respond
to him when he began to send
electrical currents
through my brain, and said to him, sweetly:
Be careful now. There is a very good
chance there is a gryphon in my brain.

I imagine all of the nurses
and assisting surgeons would flee
the room. The lead neurosurgeon
would remain rooted
to the spot, his gloved hands
arrested in mid-air. What could he do?
He might try to close up the hole
in my brain quickly,
but I would advise him not to try,
since gryphons are known as guards
and mine is certainly not a lazy gryphon,

or one erupted from a mud volcano,
or evicted from some lesser devil's
woodyard.

She is most definitely not
a geologic curiosity. She is a real gryphon,
who might be inclined to deafen
the antiseptic halls of the hospital
with her trumpet-toned voice,
were the surgeon to stop.
Considering that I would be
in a rather unsettled state, the surgeon
would have no choice
but to call back his assistants
to listen as I described
this gryphon: how she is the color
of a Mandarin garnet;
being female,
she was called *Simorgh*
in ancient Persia,
where she was divine and wise
and ate only edible flowers:
red lotus, yellow jasmine, white water lilies.

The doctors and nurses
would continue working,
interrupting my story only momentarily
in order to watch my body
levitate with delight

as the wires were placed just perfectly.
They would be relieved to see,
once that was done,
how my gryphon, tired but satisfied,
would settle her wings, fold her claws,
and lay down her heavy mammal head.

She would be ready for eternal sleep,
to once again become
a chimerical history,
having worked so hard all these years,
perched quietly on her tree of life,
shaking loose
the healing seeds.

Water from Oar

A nurse comes to my bedside,
pushes my shoulder
gently, rousing me at 3 a.m.
It's when they like to do the CT scans,
she tells me, and suddenly all the world
comes rushing back.
I can't feel my head; it's still numb.
My companion this night
is sleeping, one arm crossed
over her eyes as if she is shielding
herself from a light
she doesn't want to see.
Her hair falls in a thick knot
around her shoulders,
and I remember how it felt
in my hands after she broke her back
and I leaned over the tub
to wash out the tangles, her arms too weak
to lift the curled heft. As I washed
her hair, I could smell woodsmoke,
juniper, slickrock, perfumes
swept down with the river's
big water and the kayaks. As they wheel
me to radiology, I think
about how I'd sit for hours
on the banks of the Colorado, just to watch
her graceful rolls,

the way she separated
water from oar. Her laughter
as she plummeted under
and then sprang back upward,
split through solemn canyon walls.
I am lucky; though I have awoken
once again into tumultuousness
of illness, I feel her pushing,
pushing me to a river's
eddies, to safety.

Laurel

After the two brain surgeries,
and the implantation
of the neurostimulator
in my chest, just above my heart,
I am left alone with flowers
and food from a farmer's market.
Outside, September is still
summering. My sister is in the other room
quietly working,
and sometimes I tiptoe
out to the hallway, watch her
gazing out the window at the juniper tree.
I am restless and sore.
My head is wrapped
in a turquoise scarf
and I want to go walking. We walk
down to the pie shop,
buy coffee, animal crackers
and strawberry/rhubarb pie.
We take turns carrying the treats back
up to the house. I notice
her arms, how long and lithe
they are, how the years
of ballet classes have shaped
her body elegant
as the blue sky.
She speaks to me in the voice

of a bird:
chassé, élevé, fouetté, glissade,
and the scent of daphne
follows her,
trails me.

My sister remembers

me watching her face
in the soft cadmium orange
light of her kitchen,
just before she takes me
to the airport. She dreamt last night
about our father, how he stood
over our beds and called to us
gently when we were children,
his loneliness sweeping like frigid
wind across a glacier tarn.

We did not know why
when he drank he became frightened
of our lengthening bodies
and spoke of our transforming
as if we were not part of it.

My sister remembers
how we would hear him coming
down the hall, and, rushing to her bed,
I slipped under her arm,
a pasque flower hidden beneath snow.
She remembers how I pressed against her.

To this day, I know the female body
is a quiet space I can lean into
like entering a thicket of reeds

in water, the soft terrain
tucking me back
into the small frame
that my father, sorrowing,
could not retrieve.

II

WINGS, CREATURES & OTHER TALES

Not all bodies are recovered

–D.A. Powell

Sand Painting

I

Children from many reservations wander
through the Kir-pink light
of Santa Barbara.
They recognize borders,
walk carefully around Spanish
lavender, rockroses and golden sage.

A Lakota student watches earrings
shift under my yellow hair,
muted hematite beads
between porcupine quills.
I talk and mark her sentences
with a red pen.

She stares at me
as if my words are razors running
across her words. My red marks
are clever, they clip her language
away like a gardener cuts rose hips.
She takes it from my hands
and I know she is not going to change
a single word.

II

Four Pueblo women knock
on my dorm room door.
The metal sound of fat keys
in a fist. They want to go
walking by the sea
and I hear one say,
I'm trying to get this girl . . . but
I think she's gone AWOL.
I think of these beautiful
women, the bravery
of their long hair, scent
of piñon trees
from their high desert home.

I lie quietly on the bunk bed
until they leave.
I really want to run
after them and speak
and speak and speak
until someone can explain
how this Lakota girl
makes me disappear
when I walk by her.

I know we hear each other.
I know we listen to each other,

though from parallel corridors
that never meet.
We linger, we wait,
but even the breeze between us
carries sand.

Pelican

Under warm New Mexico sun,
we watched the pelican place
himself down among the mallards
as if he had been there all along,
as if they were expecting the large,
cumbersome body, the ungainliness.
And he, sensing his own unsightly
appearance, tucked his head close
to his body and took on the smooth,
insouciance of a swan.

Observing the Ancient

Stylemys lived at the end of the Eocene epoch, some 33-34 million years ago. Fossils were found in the Nebraska Badlands by a paleontologist in 1980.

Pieces of the carapace
fit into the palm of her hand,
the concentric circles
speaking to her from light
years away, up from shortgrass prairie
where more pieces hide
between the silvery lupine,
sagebrush and white asters.
Her fingers trace geometric
patterns and determine,
even before she knows
herself, it's just a simple tortoise
whose colors match
the colors of the sandy soil.
Piece by piece she assembles
the tortoise back to life,
as her breath imprints the air,
falls like a wreath
around the tortoise's cracked
and petrified shell
until she can almost make it move.
She sees it inching
back across the centuries

to its home in the cooling
woodlands that grew
beneath a younger star,
so faint it allowed the disarray
of ice to descend over the earth
with such ferocity
that trees cracked
and sank into bogs.
Their rings held tales,
of all the lovely creatures
who froze and were reborn
like the tortoise,
shaped and chiseled
into being, and she sees herself
as the ancient one,
rotating through the ruins, rising
from the sand,
dusting herself off,
backbone bending
into carapace,
as she begins her own slow journey
into the ages.

Twins

On the frozen pond I skated, seeking the enclosed place where layers of ice rose to the surface, rough beads of air.

Trees cracked like gunshot.

I imagined that beneath the tormented sheen of ice lay a body, with a mouth that rent the still afternoon with a hollow backhand sound so loud it left my skin bruised.

A boy in the center of the pond discovered a weak patch of ice. He flew across the emaciated glass over and over, bending its cloisonné back, pressing the dwindling bone under and under, to the amusement and amazement of children who stood in the humid, mid-winter air, their hands little nets waving, voices taunting him, urging the ice:

Swallow him whole, swallow him half, swallow him quartered, until nothing is left.

I came up behind him, cinched my arms around his waist. We flew together, twinned, and no one could pull us away from the hard hope of falling, falling into something broken, already dead.

In a Dry Summer

They are outside every window
clearing their throats
with trumpery,
haranguing for hours
at nothing more than subdued rain.

Luminous
coal wings whoosh
open,
maddening the cat
who shrinks
under the porch.

Midafternoon
they quiet down
with all the jazzy
garbling of an inebriated horde.
Rain stops too,
beats itself back up to the sky.

Insects fill the void
with spirited crescendo
weaving into fleabane.

Then, these crows
and ravens
disappear for hours,

presumably somewhere
multiplying furiously.

They return
lamenting
the night hours,
loudly, of course,
so we can all yield
to an enduring comedy
of resilience,
theirs, the best.

Descending Aria

One day you are as light
as a bird, and then
you are not.
Certain habits
clung to you: watching days
wither and how the slow
yellowing of trees repeated the lack
of love, of love, of love.

You implore the air
to let you learn
again the easy lift
of limbs no longer feathers,
but it never replies
the way the wind would.

There are some shapes
that avenge others.
The moon is one
whose semblance, when crested,
recalls lost wings,
lost language.

Beneath it, you are as lonely as
the sacrificial sparrow. Love anoints
only what is radiant; now, it sears
your flesh. How will you bear
its lost cadence,
rest without its shade?

Portents & Jesus

I remember the crab tree; a willow in the backyard.

My mother called it the crab tree;
it was where we hid the crabs in buckets.

They died quick as sand slips into the sea,
away from the salt water of their tidal pools;

we took them just to watch them wither
in the humidity beneath the willow.

When they began to smell, mother yelled
across the lawn to throw them away, but we did not.

We kept them like the winged
ants that sometimes flew into our tangled hair.

We were like those ants: squeezing
out another creature's organs, pinning

it down wretched and clawing all the way to heaven.
Under the willow tree, my sister and I

did not notice our own bodies, but sometimes Jesus
came at night, pinched us, left red bruises on our bellies.

We imagined him laughing as he pushed out our insides,
our secret egg cells once made ready for nuptial flights.

Grief of My Brothers

This is what I saw.

One brother's head slammed
against green tiles,

and bottles broken at night over
a sink, smell of liquor, overripe fruit.

One brother collected purple
salamanders, imprisoned

them in glass, contracted salmonella
and later, the jewel of sickness,

schizophrenia, that hid
for a time in its terror

clothes. One brother curled
himself under rose mallow, and fed

a crooked bird, anguish
fastened to his throat, binding

his voice until he could barely
swallow. Beside the ephemeral creek,

my brothers played and separated
one blackberry after another from

curved thorns and learned that when
the soft litany of rain returned,

they could watch the supplicant
water overwhelm its shallow basin,

overflow for days, pushing
dark matter, debris over knickpoints.

My Lithium, My Heart

Among the throngs of people rushing by,
you stand with eyes that do not meet my own.
You hear each leaf fall as you hear a sigh
of partiality, then you're alone.
I will decoupage your eyes, your blue veins,
and create speckled art from your frozen hands,
and through the length of quiet, wintery strands,
a shuttered beauty will be yours, sustained.
The frozen ground is yours to keep
pounding empty sounds to empty sleep;
you wake each day to end the endless drain.

Against the autumn sky your visage wastes.
I am part montage, part blended absence
that fits into your mind as cut and paste,
collage of patterns that you somehow sense
you once knew long ago with childish depth.
But here you stand in colors that have failed,
your spirit tightly knitted, tightly veiled—
it is your own and so I am bereft,
and pull away to leave you to the dark,
my brother, this man who holds my heart
so carelessly, it slips, and nothing's left.

Other Creatures

Sandhill cranes crowded
into shifting wind
shear where their pathos
of humming throats
seemed to conjure
the rattlesnake
we stopped short
to listen to. Then seeing
its swelling body digesting
another creature, we feared
for the one crane who flew
even as its split
leg hung useless
below the bulk of its body.
And the others—
one behind it,
one in front:
intermediaries. They knew
what we knew:
one slip of wind,
a squall line, or downburst,
and taut strands of snakes
would make their sun-sodden
journey to the center of the fields,
waiting with other maligned angels
for what might fall as fast
as blood falls
from a severed throat.

Story from an Iñupiaq Sewing Kit

A woman looks out onto the vast,
near-frozen tundra of an arctic headland.

She holds her heart like she holds
her bird-bone needle case,

tucked tightly into silence,
while early hoarfrost settles

around her shoulders and hair.
She threads sinew through pieces

of tanned animal leather. She hurries—
her husband and the salmon

will not wait and he needs the new
atigi, the hood of it from the wolverine,

whose glossy fur scatters
the radiance of ice back

into the wind where it wandered
and fell through the woman's dreams.

The ice woke her early and she knew
to sew an amulet of gratitude

onto the sleeve of the lining,
so her husband would be safe

as he set out to look for salmon,
his spear soon piercing

the plated scales of the fish,
reaching the soft inner flesh, reminding him

of the flesh of the woman
and her stories. When he lays

his head down, he waits
for the dark nights to come, hears

the quiet pull of the needle
through material as this woman

works her words into each stitch
as carefully as if she were separating

the spinal cord of the fish
from the pink meat.

He watches as she sews a circle.
In centuries, the ice will close

over everything he loves, leaving
their bones frozen,
mutating into permafrost.

Desolation Beauty

Say's Phoebe (Sayornis saya) and House Finch
(Carpodacus mexicanus) nest, found in Boulder,
Colorado, 1903

These eggs like pearls or glass beads, split
from some other time. From some other hand,
their nest is drawn down from trees the winds knit
in restless movement on a montane land.
The eggs are what the centuries speak of, plainly:
something, somewhere makes us ponder why
the constant perish is a sharp refrain
that shuts our hearts so we can deny
what is taken from us cannot be returned.
Into this fragile landscape I place my story;
a time on tundra when I found a nest, spurned,
as if it had been waiting just for me.
A lark's two blue eggs shone,
dead and abandoned; I left them alone.

Weathered

Those boys must have learned
to bear the Wyoming wind
from snow fences bent along
the highway, from fields flat as their eyes,
no asylum from tides of antelope skirring
through frozen needle-and-thread, followed
by the scud of grifters,
hypothermic vultures. Beating him
to death, they were like children
who had learned first the burn
of wind, then to turn a cold cheek, hands
cupping ears to block the sound
of a wind with no beginning,
no end. How many times they kept at it
they can't remember,
only that he had always been
with them, part of that wind,
the one intimate sibling.

Wing Medicine

When the body is beginning
to weaken, it pays attention
to the creature it hopes to become.
I'm standing in January
twilight wrapped in wool sweaters,
watching a moon leavening
wetlands and cattails.
Snow geese inscribe the sky,
followed by sandhill cranes
whose wings are tidal:
the sound of water seeking water.
Bone follows bone,
wing follows wing.
In such configuration they must speak
to one another: *Wherever you go,*
I will go.
Corded together, they fan, expand,
shed feathers over fields, far
mesas, riparian forests.
In marshes, herons and coots
wade, rust willows waver
and I hear the undulate heartbeats
of blackbirds, roadrunners, pheasants.
Winged ones, taking flight in multitudes,
in shapes I once failed to recognize.

Flight Patterns

I know about the creatures
who are changed
in one way or another;
I am one. I don't need a Talmudic
blessing. I keep my internal
motion to myself. I keep
my external motion
in check with pills
and leads braided through my head,
down through my neck,
into my chest.
At the airport, a security guard
runs her hands up and down
my body checking for some invisible
device. She tells me with a solemn
face that she is deriving no pleasure
from this body search.
A man standing across the aisle
waiting for his shoes
to slide down the security
conveyor belt,
watches as my breasts are touched,
gently. I look up at him
and he smiles at me, delighted.
On the plane, I am seated tightly
against the window and feel crowded
by the woman next to me:

she might sense a tremor.
I am thankful for the turbulence,
the rocking, the insistent lurch as the plane
lifts itself from what is solidly true
for something no one can
rationally explain. This height
is perilous and peculiar.
I close my eyes and see
myself from another height,
released at last from
the body, my dust settling
over winterfat, then swept
up again to land
across the backs of sandhill cranes
where I am once again lifted
and moving.

Bullet Suicide

When I count, there are only you and I together
But when I look ahead up the white road
There is always another one walking beside you
  –T.S. Eliot

The bullet scrapes your ear,
falls to your feet,
makes a red knot.
Your hands tremble as the cricket
trills below the rough terrain
of sky—sky of warriors, and arrows
that drop silver. The tundra
is a loneliness too, and you
must cross its swelling
of displaced marsh water.
You walk across it with another,
fanning out across time-honored soil,
seeking slaughtered Ute shadows.
If you slip
from a snow-covered precipice,
you will die. You know
this is terrain of demented angels.
You cannot stop yourself.
You go on up
until you are nearly touching
the cold sky that will never end.
You know already

you will be walking this trail
with the other beside you,
until morning mirrors
the yellow avens you lay
your head down onto now to rest.

Disappearances

Little then,
my children,
who with deft feet nearly flew

pushed upward through night air
where they grew
into their evanescent bones.

Far below them lay
the tossed and quiet husks
of flower skin, pale cartilage.

I watched my children,
their triumphs rising and I,
clamoring over barriers, followed.

Around me it seemed
familiar footholds
slipped away as easily as lichen

eroded and fell
into alluvial pools.
Reverberate sounds

of water conversed, filled,
and I could only wait
while every season caught

the bodies of my children,
rearranging them
until smallness was irretrievably gone.

I looked again and tried to remember
who took them,
who stole them,

who gathered them
like bright seed leaf to be
scattered across the farthest field
to inaudible corners
where all things change in quiet.

Grendel's Loss Again

Grendel's mother, monster of women, mourned her woe.
She was doomed to dwell in the dreary waters, cold sea-
courses. . . .

– from Beowulf

Three black bears appeared on my deck
without a sound.
5:00 a.m.
I watched them through glass doors,
recalling chokecherries
encircling our house.

The cubs stood on their hind legs,
small paws pressed against the glass.
They saw me, but through their blurry vision,
I was nothing more than pale seedstalk.

The sow finally smelled me
and her whole auburn-shining body hardened.
She turned her heavy head and in minutes had
ambled silently down the flagstone stairs,
past the wild iris and poppies.
Her cubs followed reluctantly.
They came back up;
they went back down.

The mother was not killed in a home
beneath tumultuous waters
by a warrior out for revenge,
but because she stole birdseed
from someone's deck.

Tempted, the bear licked up linseed,
flaxseed, hayseeds with such greed,
hoarding them while her cubs slept safe.

She was trapped one evening by the DOW
in a steel, tin-can contraption and
screamed all night in her tight prison,
surrounded by the smells of other slaughtered animals.

Her voice punctured every tree,
perforated walls
of every house in the valley.

The ranger came in the morning
and we heard the loud crack of his .45
that he placed strategically
through a side trap door.

He shot her mercifully through the head.
When he opened the trap,
he saw that she had torn out all
her claws and teeth.

Modor, who were you?
ides, āglæc-wīf, mere-wīf, āglæc-wīf
In scholarly books, they still argue over
your role. Such a creature you were
and your children are diminishing.

I saw only one of them again,
grown old enough to forage for himself.
But when he came to the door
and tipped his head up to me,
I could have suckled him.

Instead, I picked up hefty moss rocks and,
my boys following,
we chased him back, back
into the woods, battering
him with glinty rose-quartz weapons
until he cried out in misery,
and disappeared forever.

Burial Burlesque

*In 2002, northwest Georgia's Tri-State Crematory
operators were brought to court after officials found
over 300 corpses stacked in sheds, others half-buried. In
order to identify the bodies, many family members were
subjected to picking through decomposing remains.*

In a forest in Georgia beneath canopied trees
(*What does your body say about your soul?*)
name tags were slipped around feet and knees.

Roses and corpses entwined near a shed
(*They flew apart in disorder*)
your body among them, moss near your head.

Softwood, your bones dissolving in soil,
(*One must have chaos in one*)
their decomposition a silence unspoiled.

Your daughters searched through a tapestry of leaves
(*The air thin and pure*)
skimming the ground when the wind would grieve.

Each daughter went home, full of regrets,
(*Then the wings of their spirit broke*)
your death a burlesque casting dark silhouettes.[1]

---

1   Middle lines italicized from *Thus Spoke Zarathustra* by Friedrich
Nietzsche

66

III

BOUQUETS, FEASTS & FLUTES

Beautiful my desire and the place of my desire.

– Theodore Roethke

Sweetgrass and the Art of Bicycle Maintenance

I was old enough to be
his mother. I watched his body move
like sweetgrass in spring,
and he smiled as he bent over
to run his hands,
brown as maple sugar, along my
tires to make sure they were true.
Squatting down to inspect
my chain, his thighs spread
wide, bone and muscles lengthening
under low-slung khaki shorts.
Each one of his fingers touched
the stain of what was left
of the oil as he lifted it gently,
black smudges migrating up
to his temples as he brushed back
his long, amber hair.
I was happy to let him
fix everything. When the bike was ready,
my tongue became smooth
as a pearl when I called him over
to adjust the seat again. He leaned
near me, and his skin smelled like the sun
on slickrock sand. His arms
were long and when he stood, I could hear
the murmur in his ribs.

Mothers of boys are dangerous.
We have pressed our mouths against the small flesh
that came from us, extracting ambrosia
from flowers only we can find.
He was so beautiful, I was afraid
to speak. If I opened my mouth,
yew berries, little mariposa souls
would have rattled out instead of words.

The Lovely Feast

The dreams remind you
of how you were born again
under a juniper tree, smoky perfume
and sap sticking to your body.

They keep coming every night
from places you have forgotten.
You wake from them, reluctantly, cold
mountain breezes tangling your hair.

They wrest you down with the same force
of that boy who held you
hard, only half a man yet.
How he brought his mouth to your
mouth, and the taste of what he had
discovered was something you thought forbidden,
something you thought you could never love.

People of God want to know
about epiphanies, but when you tell them,
they stutter and burn,
simple-minded disciples.

Language you thought was a lost dialect
comes back to you soft and slow
as you slip back, remembering how easily
the juniper berries were crushed
as he forced you to open, and with your opening,
the fierce baptism you had been waiting for.

Le Sirenuse

(The little islands)

The neighborhood ladies
had slender ankles,
rounded contours
shifting near my mother's garden
where wild mint grew,
the wild mint my mother snipped
to float in glasses of summer tea.

The ladies who came to gossip
were umber from seaside sun,
their lipstick and nail polish
reflected all the colors
of the whirling planets, even Saturn's
scattering hues.
But my mother wore no makeup
and her skin was opalescent,
eyes blue, belly always slightly plump
from her many children.

The women formed circles
into which young girls
could slyly wedge.
Sometimes we watched
as they played mah-jongg
late into the afternoon, tiles clicking
like castanets through dark-colored leaves.

One woman wore a sunflower
print dress that rose above her brown knees.
She taught my sister and me to walk
straight as magazine models
by balancing a book on our heads.

Somewhere near us there was an ocean
my mother was afraid
to swim in, but she could sing
its mystic tales. At night, voice half-bird, half-woman,
my mother pulled us under to sleep,
but not before her singing stopped and I believed
somewhere there had been a little death.

Redress

Flesh, our one possession, the heart is its own redress.
–Matthew Cooperman

A doctor peers at x-rays
and sees every day
what she fears: spalled
bones, mass on a skull, small spills
of mutated cells.
At night she envisions these things
change, that in the morning
she will bring a patient
in a milk-blue gown news
that all is well,
everything just a flower
rendered transparent.
Her hand covers the patient's hand
and together they look
at radiographed rose petals,
wavy bivalves floating
on an invisible watercourse,
engrailed bracts in a spring
cold snap, serried bells,
the throat of an amaryllis
a resurrection bursting
mountain fire's plain pearls, bracken.
Someone down the long hall
calls out *"Butcherbird, butcherbird,"*

as if in warning,
but the patient is already beginning
her lonely walk
toward the distant desert
where she can rest,
red soil beneath her feet,
pulling her in and in.

The Bouquet of Desire

For Claire and Audrey Emma

Just two hours old
you lie in my arms,
small niece,
your heart beating
fast as a wren's breath.

I breathe in your little perfume
of antique porcelain
encased in sleep;
you've been here before

and know I will hold you
next to your mother
who moans gently
in sleep,
remembering the pummeling
of bones that expanded
to make a path.

And here you are:
honeysuckle your hands,
who can say where they've been?

Your mother wakes,
I can barely hand you over—
maybe she will not share you again

and I will be lost in that abyss:
an aging auntie,
releasing her silent eggs
into the womb memory,
irretrievable red bell.

Milk & Roses

At first, you and I are lost
in a burnt, impoverished limber pine
forest above timberline that moves
when no one sees, inching leeward
as though seeking
water, a sea, in anguish.

You and I seek each other
under a moon
that leads us blindly
from rain shadow
to rain shadow,
from green-yellow banner
trees, one-sided silhouettes
braced to clamorous wind.

You and I move
through this labyrinth.
You slip far ahead,
and a peculiar light trails
your heart, creates an empty chamber
where I wish to deposit mine.

But you will not allow this.
As you climb closer
to air that can only stop breath,
I have no strength to stop you.

My hands are empty.
But you have given me gifts,
left behind garlands and wreaths of roses,
spilling sweet like milk
from my breasts.

Taking Pleasure

The city opens in cadence of light
and along the roads of Port-au-Prince
I travel, looking for paintings.
Near sewage seeping,
I am offered sugared
café torréfié garanti pur
in a hotel that arranges bird cages
by fountains and marble stairs. In gardens,
windy fuchsias tap my cheeks.
In galleries, I buy paintings of obese Haitians;
immense limbs
crowded into *tap taps,*
arms full, baskets
of calabash, coconut, mango
pressed between plump ankles.
Evening, and I lift my face
to ceiling fans in a restaurant
hidden in the hills of Pétion-Ville.
A young man dances me
to the veranda where rain-breeze
sweetens between my thighs.
Next to us a tour guide holds
a French woman in his arms,
he smooths back her hair and he tells us
the Duvaliers were good people:
"If you were in the system, you had nothing to fear."

Below us, a man with a machine gun winks.
He knows all our desires
and protects us from the outside:
wire stretched across limestone walls;
stacks of burning tires blocking roads;
the children I've held each year in clinics,
caressing their arms as if to lure parasites away,
cradling orbed stomachs
as if to subdue hunger with my fingers.

The Wintering of Panama

Her quiet pain comes
as together you watch
snow fall quietly in November.
All the birds are gone,
she says, and you tell her:
No, they are still here:
rosy winter finches, gray jays, chickadees.
You show your fragile mother-in-law
how to find pine cones,
to bend down, pick them carefully
from around prickly pear,
cover them with suet
and sunflower seeds,
how to place
them around her deck in feeders.
This way her aching
for Panama, the absence of green,
will not burden
her mind quite so much.
You make her soup,
then she wants to lie down
surrounded by her Christmas
cactus hanging heavy
with its lavender
blooms. You can leave her now.
She is fine, her sorrow
caught in colors, and the remaining

birds that will wake her
in the morning with song.
You imagine her one good eye opening
to sounds of her lost children,
returning from cloud forests,
dusty roads,
banana leaves flickering
in the small gusts
of their hands.

Bodega Bay

Fog and kites open the morning. They wisp across the sky, billowing over sand dunes. Your children are still small and you look up from your sleeping bag to gauge the deep Pacific's sound. Is it the unmistakable sound of undertow, or sleeper waves? These things you can recognize—children in Haiti would stand still over the coral cove and gaze hard at the blue water, watching, listening and would cry out if you attempted to jump in, *"Pas nager! Pas nager!"*

Half-asleep, you mumble to the warm bodies of your sons lying next to you, *"Pas nager."* Incense of eucalyptus trees, the chinook-like wind, and someone cooking on a grill make you push back the wool blankets, crawl out of the sleeping bag, squeeze silently out of the tent, and there before you is the tumultuous Pacific, so unlike the placid Atlantic that you grew up near; near enough to ride your bike to, and later, when you were a teenager, to hitchhike to. The ocean was useful to you, then; you took off your jeans and soaked them in the ocean, then laid them on the sand, in the sun. They would fade naturally and you would look so nonchalant at parties with those jeans, salt-bleached and faded a softer blue than any ocean you'd seen so far.

Here, on Bodega Bay there are many birds, of course. They careen. You watch them and think how lucky they are, these creatures. They fly far above any ground and into the world. You love their sound, a sound of wind being sliced through invisible tree branches. They remind you over and over again of so many different oceans you have been in and of your teenage years and then, of course, they remind you of your own children. You turn and stumble back to the warm tent where you will pleasure in the weight of their bodies against yours for just a few more years and this realization becomes a riptide, dragging you back into a netherworld sleep.

Little Apple

I

A woman gazing
in the mirror sees behind her
a window opening

out into the garden:
there, a blue heron
absorbs a fuchsia light.

II

A woman wading
into tide pools, grass beds,
searches for the insatiable

sea stars. She coaxes those
shorn from their salt marshes
to endure a new surface.

III

A woman touching
the branch of a manzanita,
desires its color

for herself; she breaks
off one limb, its red husk so like
a garnet fastened to the sun.

IV

A woman observing
each entity's quiet enterprise
covets all,

her own body
unable to capture such
elemental beauty unrestrained.

The Healers

From the very beginning they came,
bearing the rosaries of snow.

One had the palsied foot
and leaned toward you, stamping
the ground, declaring you would see fire
when you were just a child and knew nothing.

You looked down at your Easter dress
and the ribbons quivered.
It was the first time you could make things move
with fear.

* * *

One day, in Missouri, a very old black man
approached you in a bus station
and whispered, *Be careful,*
your heart is in your eyes.

His hands took your hands and they were like ash,
and you watched as his face disappeared
into the crowds of rapture
where others, too, were carried away and marked.

* * *

This time, you have asked to be healed.
Oil, candlelight, and incense form a safe
paradise, and hands slide down your head
like your father brushing your hair.

Somehow you can't hear their prayers.
You hear the pleading, the insistence,
but your prayer is your own:

Five seeds inside an apple form a flower.
I have seen this with my eyes
and traced the tiny pockets with my fingers.
It is forming a rose.

       * * *

A good friend tells you secrets of a harp:
lean against one,
letting amiable fingers thread a timbre
and the draining dopamine will return.
There are rules, of course:
the body must first remember to move
like a child: *my thin arms to and fro.*

Others take you to watch cranes
migrate and you hear them speaking
to you from an impenetrable height
as they till the sky.

A cool leaf slips from your heart
as you try to follow,
your arms outstretched beneath them.

* * *

Illness is the smallest of ancient planets,
building its tiers in the sky piece by piece.
Far below, you have no warning
when it finally manifests itself
as quietly as a rose,
the resin of its garnet mouth
singing, it too, a healing,
reminding you of what you have
known forever.

At the Alhambra

It is spring, and I drift through vestiges of Moors,
and stop to look over parapets at miles
of whitewashed houses without discernible doors,
as if to enter Spain's past one must embrace denial.
Yet beauty brings me to an intimate barrier
and Granada's pastoral scenery sighs
with mayapples, lavender and lush wisteria.
And then some hallowed voice inside me cries:
it does not bother me now to know
I'm filled with a disease that's moving me
to a center that may be as cold as snow,
and I will arrive there gratefully.
Some think with a peculiar point of view:
my blood's roses, under Allah's eyes, grew.

Doubting Cremation

Six months since you died
and only now I begin to feel
the missing resonance of your body.

I walk for hours through fresh snow;
the ground is a rib I turn over
with each step. I unearth
what should not be on this earth
but is familiar to me. I unearth you.

Then, we walk through ponderosa pines
and they begin creaking in the wind.
I mistake them for the sound of your
child voice, like the lilt of a flute
leading me to the taproot
where I stop to rest beneath
boles and branches.

I know you will eventually become
as ancient as they, and I grow heavy
with thoughts of your missing body,
your body burned away
to gray ash, impossible to hold.
Then, you leave me again.

What rose up from your burning
was not only severance of skin from bone,

tissue from flesh, tendon from muscle,
but the beauty of a body
torn twice from mine, because all mothers
repeat the births of their children who die.

Sometimes I am lucky
and find you, clamoring just enough
so that I momentarily rejoice and rejoice,
my hands opening to hold you again
as carefully as I might hold the lavender
butterfly loosened from its gambel oak.

Gully Wash

The neurosurgeon's hands are steady;
he switches the drill off and on,
just to make sure that what he is hearing
is the sound-shatter of bones,
a wash of sand down
a long gully,
a thousand pins dropping onto stone.

In his world,
staples announce patience.
Scissors sharpen with empathy.
Tissue is swiftly sewn together;
the air around an opening stitched closed—a circle.

In the other close world,
the spirit unfastens itself as though
it is readying to leave its person behind,
to promenade blithely as a string of lace
over fierce terrain, each eyelet
an open prayer.

River Tales

For Mary Jean

There was one morning
when the slow metrical plane
of the Tennessee River
was so calm,
I imagined I could see
where it began
and where it ended.
Its supine surface shone obsidian.
I distrust a body
of water that is silent,
want to hear sound
of wave against shore
or stone, and the steady
thump of a listless log
knocking against a pier's
strongholds.
I distrust a body
of water appearing benign.

That morning,
I wanted the dock
I was standing on to unloosen
itself and move
with a quick current,

past the sweet gum
branches trailing
like broken spines
near the shallows.
I looked up and saw others
on the far bank,
heard muffled voices
caught in the quirky mishap
of having been summoned
from their infinities
unexpectedly.

I recognized the voices
of my grandmothers: both girls
again, making river and earth
around them tilt
with their ruckus,
and I left my body
to drift beside them,
listening, remembering
chimes, bells and charms
that only girls can cast
out like handfuls of sugar
across any universe,
any threshold.
They pulled me in with them
and I heard them laughing:
This is where we come.
This is where we come.

August

Dry moon wanders sky
searches for the one cool edge
where heat breaks its neck

His Death

What should I put into this piece about you, my son?
Half the time I am rinsing the dishes, doing laundry
(some of which pops up occasionally as yours); the
other half of time I spend wondering how it happened
that you slipped from my hands and became white
ashes. At least I seem to think of your burnt bones
as enmeshed with some monochromatic hue. Often,
while walking the dog through late winter snow, I hear
your voice, uncharacteristically cheerful, once again
a child at the school fair, holding a balloon whose
circumference of color is larger and more buoyant than
your wide, blue eyes—the same eyes that stared up at
me from where you slid to the floor during one of the
moments, the infinitesimal seconds of a seizure. How
hard is marble? How hard is gray slate? They are hard
enough so that I put my hands beneath your head and
cried out to the empty house for help. No one ever
came. Then your eyes refocused and were fixed onto
mine, once again calm, and prophetically sightless.

One day, you disappeared and then reappeared far
across a street. Yes, this was a dream, but no matter the
distance, you came as a boy during the time you were
my milk and honey, your small body still anchored
to mine. The intimacy of your breath was like honey
too, and your hair, your skin. What part of your body
really came from me? Surely not this ethereal skin
that is ash now, your skin that I could feel tightly
stamped against mine for what passed as centuries, and
was ancient, discernible only through the immutable
strangeness of love. Stars in their strangeness feel their

way in shifting configurations over an ocean, only to slip and drown alone, and miraculously. You did not drown, but one bright morning, you skimmed across an ocean and drifted like stars too many to count. Everything must have been so quiet for you, and miraculous. You drifted and were swept off, then must have learned to speak through dreams to tell me this: *over and over again, over and over again, Mom.* I keep trying to discern what it is you are telling me. Unbearable, unbearable your death.

In many dreams I am swimming in an ocean. I have been swimming in this same ocean my entire life. I wake feeling the undertow pulling my legs, wake feeling the sand banks dissolving beneath my feet, wake hearing the perpetuity of wave after wave. Always, when I walk in the mountains, I mistake the constant shush of wind as a nearby ocean. To rest or calm myself, I imagine I am floating in a cove in Haiti, just a little way off from a coral reef. You are there again with me, and we are floating together, and discussing the presence of tiger sharks. Haitian children pull us up and out of the water. Their long, thin arms pull us up over the sharp coral, and we are newly baptized, and you say, *We have to take care of each other, Mom.*

Over and over again.

Must we repeat each death? I could bear another's grief, and have. I have studied the faces of the newly dead. I have studied the faces of those who loved them. In all of their faces there is an immutability that resonates. It is the immutability of things repeating.

The universe bears no flatness. Even its horizon is curved toward repetition. Your death is a horizon. I run to slip over its edge. I long to slip over its edge. I am not afraid because I have studied immutability and love—how they keep the silent heart locked in its narrow antechamber, the place where we believe we keep the dead. But we do not keep them, they keep us, torn, in love, and again, in love.

Some Small Thing I Have Held

Early morning light narrows
through windows,
pulling cold moon scars
across pinyon pine floors.
I walk quietly downstairs,
balancing myself like an egg
in someone else's hands.

In a room below,
my teenage son and his girlfriend
sleep. I imagine them curled saplings,
leaves enfolded.

The door to my son's room is shut.
I shouldn't open it,
but I have something to tell her:
Your mother called, asking,
Is my daughter there?

I open the door just enough
to see her slide from his chest,
like a thin strand of gold,
then hide under his arm,
one eye open.

I draw back, close the door.
Some small thing I have held

slips from my hands,
vanishes under it.

I stand outside ashamed
to have seen anything at all,
still breathless from the wind
my son was born in.

Oread Speaks to the River at Dusk

I was a girl in Mytilene. The caress
of sun upon my face woke me to morning's
first goldenrod flush and I learned to give thanks
for these gifts of love.

I gathered the watery papyri
and lotus from beneath a topaz moon
that lit the wooded path to my lover,
who gave me sweet wine.

When he first came to me, he took precedence
over the listless stars, and I allowed this
because he brought me dill and dark-red roses,
unbraided my hair,

and unclasped my sandals, and I recognized
the balm of twilight in his eyes. He drew the
sea down over me until the Pleiades moved;
I was not ashamed.

It was my brothers who urged me to climb far
up the Leucadian cliffs, farther than I
had ever been and I fell, and still fell
believing I had transformed,
and the husk of my body was left behind.

Crocosmia and Plum

Suzanne wore white shirts crisp
from the dry cleaners and black wrap skirts.

She was small, with dark
petal fingers that held coins and strings

of snow peas she snapped in half
during winter afternoons while I read

grammar books and waited to seat
people who came to eat by fountains

and glass fish arranged along a wall. Late
nights after dancing with men who pulled

our skirts up around our thighs
and asked us to come home with them,

we reeled through new snow,
laughing, milky timbre shushing footsteps.

We drank into the morning and slept
together not knowing where our hands

should touch. Her apartment was so quiet,
cats walking across our bellies;

around us Eudora Welty books
lay open on tables.

I could imagine her lips detailing
each word as she read,

even her fingertips shivering
as she turned the pages

with love; and I imagined,
could I ever touch her, my throat

would open, the taste of plum and saffron
in my mouth, fiery, a field of crocosmia.

How tender her skin, I thought,
how thin the membrane

of her lids as they shut against
the morning's dry savannah light.

Composition of Water, Dreams & Wounds

In the desert, my husband rode
his mountain bike
around the earth's colonizer
of cyanobacteria and stayed on single track,
sometimes lingering in arroyos
to listen to the sustained
compression of wind.

He took me to Milan to see
mountain bikes as light aluminum
phantasmic machines. We walked
to shops and bought sweet things,
fucked during long afternoons
when everyone in Italy stops working
and drinks wine.

Dreams dissipating, the study
of microeconomics came to him
and he learned how to dynamite
whole mountainsides
for vacuous houses.
He taught me the parlance
of his work: fresh cut
pine and fir, giant
spools of wire, hickory
handled hammers, gold door
hardware from Brazil.

I learned where nails went and whispered
their names and needs at night in his ear:
slanted, collated pneumatic gun nails
need pneumatic tool oil.
He built us a new house,
showed me stacked sheets
of white foam
insulation that would keep us warm in winter,
cool in summer.
I learned how a builder needs a knot
of thick safety rope with a harness.
I recognized a box of silver
concrete anchors,
how the long, steel rods hold
decks and sill plates down.
I could identify a yellow soldering torch
and a chop saw.
Sometimes, I would stand in the middle
of the scattered floor observing
miscellaneous pipes and nests of wire;
stained log posts propped
into corners, shovels and brooms
leaned against framing.
I watched him work
with his hands,
thought of him writing
stories about building instead of bikes.

Days before we moved
into the house,
we watched the sky
shift quietly into dusk and he held
his hand out to me.
He guided me in the darkening
light around to the back
because there were no front
steps. He took off
his work gloves, I took his hand,
trailed my fingers
across his coarsened palm,
over nicks, cuts, places where
he had inadvertently
slipped and something
had pierced him.

I thought: there has to be
a room somewhere
in my body that can hold all
disappointments, desires.
I chose my mouth
and he opened it right there,
with his tongue
spreading my legs to taste
my sadness,
as we are composed of
salt and water,
as we are composed of wounds.

Barbara Ellen Sorensen is former senior editor of *Winds of Change* magazine, the flagship publication for the American Indian Science & Engineering Society. She now freelances for *The Tribal College Journal* and writes for the National Indian Child Welfare Association.

Sorensen's chapbook, *Song from the Deep Middle Brain* (Mainstreet Rag, 2010), was a 2011 Colorado Book Award finalist.

Sorensen was nominated for a Pushcart Prize for her memoir piece, *Ghostflower & Wind* (Drunken Boat, 2012), and an interview with her can be found in *Fringe* magazine's archived spring 2012 edition. Her undergraduate degree in English is from the University of Iowa; her graduate degree in creative writing is from Regis University.

ALSO FROM ABLE MUSE PRESS

Ben Berman, *Strange Borderlands - Poems*

Michael Cantor, *Life in the Second Circle - Poems*

Catherine Chandler, *Lines of Flight - Poems*

Maryann Corbett, *Credo for the Checkout Line in Winter - Poems*

Margaret Ann Griffiths, *Grasshopper - The Poetry of M A Griffiths*

Ellen Kaufman, *House Music - Poems*

Carol Light, *Heaven from Steam - Poems*

April Lindner, *This Bed Our Bodies Shaped - Poems*

Frank Osen, *Virtue, Big as Sin - Poems*

Alexander Pepple (Editor), *Able Muse Anthology*

Alexander Pepple (Editor), *Able Muse - a review of poetry, prose & art*
    (semiannual issues, Winter 2010 onward)

James Pollock, *Sailing to Babylon - Poems*

Aaron Poochigian, *The Cosmic Purr - Poems*

Hollis Seamon, *Corporeality - Stories*

Stephen Scaer, *Pumpkin Chucking - Poems*

Matthew Buckley Smith, *Dirge for an Imaginary World - Poems*

Wendy Videlock, *The Dark Gnu and Other Poems*

Wendy Videlock, *Nevertheless - Poems*

Richard Wakefield, *A Vertical Mile - Poems*

www.ablemusepress.com

CPSIA information can be obtained
at www.ICGtesting.com
Printed in the USA
FFOW05n1033141013
2043FF